KNOWLEDGE ENCYCLOPEDIA
ELECTRICITY & ELECTRONICS

© Wonder House Books 2021

All rights reserved. No part of this book may be reproduced or transmitted in any form by any means, electronic or mechanical, including photocopying and recording, or by any information storage and retrieval system except as may be expressly permitted in writing by the publisher.

(An imprint of Prakash Books)

contact@wonderhousebooks.com

Disclaimer: The information contained in this encyclopedia has been collated with inputs from subject experts. All information contained herein is true to the best of the Publisher's knowledge.

ISBN : 9789354401923

Table of Contents

Our Electric World	3
Gadget Mania	4–5
Electricity: The Basics	6–7
Current and Resistance	8–9
Making Electricity	10–11
Inside a Power Plant	12–13
Electric Circuits	14–15
Motors and Magnetism	16–17
Semiconductors	18–19
Diodes and Displays	20–21
Interesting Electrical Phenomena	22–23
Analogue and Digital	24–25
Making Computers	26–27
Mobile Phones	28–29
Renewable Energy	30–31
Word Check	32

OUR ELECTRIC WORLD

Think of what your house might have been like more than a hundred and fifty years ago. Mentally take out each electrical object and replace it with something that was done the old-fashioned way. Think of lanterns that burned whale oil in the living room, washing tubs with wooden bats or kitchens with coal stoves. You would have travelled on foot, or in carts pulled by horses or bullocks. You would have to write a letter to someone living far away, and it would be weeks before the letter reached them and you received a reply.

Archaeologists have divided human history into three ages—the Stone Age, the Bronze Age, and the Iron Age. While each of these ages is based on changes that drove the evolution of society, nothing changed humanity more profoundly than the ability to harness electricity for its needs. It has helped us overcome our bodies' limitations, so we can talk to someone a continent away or travel safely at night.

Let's explore the world we have created in just a hundred years!

▼ Electricity is part of our lives in ways that we often don't recognise

Gadget Mania

The air-conditioning in our homes, cars and offices, the mobile phones we use to stay in touch with the world, the electric lights that help us stay awake far into the night and drive safely on roads, and, not to forget, the toaster that magically turns slices of bread into delicious toast! We've gotten so used to electricity that we can't even imagine what to do if there is a sudden blackout. So before we look into electricity, how it works, and how it helps us in our lives, let's have a look at some of the most interesting gadgets that were ever invented.

▶ *Different rooms in your house are filled with different devices. How many can you count?*

Electrical, Electronic and Electromechanical Devices

All the gadgets we use are of three types:

1. **Electrical devices:** These convert electrical energy into light or heat, like an incandescent light bulb or water heater; or they convert light into electricity, like a solar panel. Devices like transformers, capacitors, and high voltage electric lines are also electrical devices, because they store or transport electricity without converting it into any other kind of energy.

2. **Electromechanical devices:** These convert electricity into mechanical energy (kinetic or potential energy). Ceiling and table fans, vinyl record players, dial telephones, and electric bells are examples of such devices. Devices that convert mechanical energy into electricity, like the **turbines** in dams or the blades of windmills, are also electromechanical devices.

3. **Electronic devices:** These are devices that use complex electrical circuits, where '**gates**' change the flow of electricity to create different outputs. Televisions, computers, and mobile phones are all electronic devices. They often involve tinier gadgets inside them that may be electrical or electromechanical devices. For example, televisions have tiny mechanical vibrators that convert electrical signals into sound signals, so that you can not only see what your favourite stars are doing in the movie you're watching, but hear them too.

▲ *Electronic, electromechanical, and electrical devices*

Isn't It Amazing!

There are some devices that we can wear, like earphones for listening to music or a smart watch that can tell us a lot more than just the time. Some people, like soldiers and firefighters, have electric jackets that adjust the temperature and glasses that take photos. In the future, we might see many electric devices become light enough to wear, rather than weigh down our pockets.

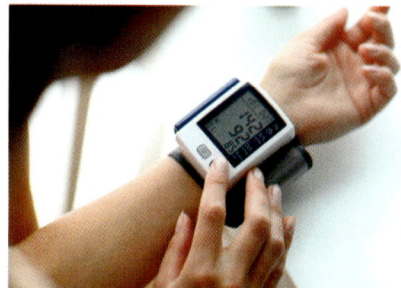

▲ *Wearable electronics can even measure your pulse rate*

Incredible Individuals

While Thomas Alva Edison is famous for inventing the electric light, did you know that the first electric light used for streets was invented by Humphry Davy? He is also known for inventing the Miners' Safety Lamp (or the Davy Lamp)

SCIENCE | ELECTRICITY & ELECTRONICS

Gadgets We've Forgotten

In the 1890s, Nikola Tesla and Thomas Edison invented rival systems to distribute electricity to homes, using alternating current and direct current respectively. Ever since then, electricity became a cheaper way of providing energy for a home's needs, compared to oil or gas for lighting lamps and kitchen fires. Inventors began to make electric devices to do all kinds of jobs, from machines that wash clothes and keep food cool, to electric fans and lawnmowers. Electricity could also help us do things we could never do before, like speak to people in a different city, or listen to a famous singer over and over again.

Today, electronics have replaced many devices that were popular with earlier generations. Vinyl records came first and were popular from the 1920s-70s, then it was cassette tapes from the 1970s-2000s, and finally, it was compact discs from the 1990s-2010s. Devices that could play these media rose in parallel, especially portable versions such as the famous Walkman™. Here are other examples:

1. **Gramophones:** These were the first devices that could play music. They consisted of a turntable, on which the listener placed a vinyl record. A gramophone pin sensed the slight differences in the grooves on the record and converted that into sound.

2. **Jukeboxes:** These were machines that would let you select and play music by inserting coins into them. They were wildly popular from the 1930s to the 1950s.

3. **Cassettes and Compact Discs (CDs):** Cassettes worked like vinyl records, but used magnetic tape instead of grooves and plastic etchings. An electromagnetic head in the player would move up and down based on the magnetic charges and convert them into sound. CDs approached this using miniature bumps and lasers.

4. **Video Cassettes:** These were similar to cassette tapes, except that they could play video as well as audio. They made it possible for people to watch their favourite movies and TV shows at home. As these cassettes were comparatively expensive, video rental stores became common throughout the world from the 1970s to the 1990s. People would borrow movies just as we can borrow books from libraries. Rental stores died out with the increased accessibility of inexpensive Digital Video Discs (DVDs) in the 2000s.

▲ *The Grammy Awards, which are given every year to top musicians, are named after the gramophone, which was invented by Thomas Edison*

▲ *Jukeboxes were common in restaurants and haircutting salons, and many retro-themed restaurants have them specially made today*

◀ *To play a video cassette, one had to load it into a special device called a video cassette player (VCP), which in turn had to be connected to the TV*

▲ *Cassettes and portable cassette players made it possible for people to listen to their favourite music wherever they went. The Sony Walkman™ sold 385 million devices from 1979 to 2010*

Electricity: The Basics

Before we learn how our devices work, let's understand what electricity is. For that we need to understand a few terms of physics. All electricity can be divided into two: static and current. **Static electricity** is what happens when your woollen clothes rub against rubber, or when lightning strikes the ground. This is because of opposite electric charges on them, as we will see ahead. **Current electricity** is what we commonly call electricity; it's 'current' because it is always on the move (dynamic). Both depend on a fundamental property of all things on Earth—an **electric charge**. Electric charges exist because of electrons, the tiny things that move around the nuclei of atoms.

Charge

Different materials have different charges on them. These charges arise because there are electrons on the surface of every atom, which move around the nucleus. Very often, these charges are balanced by an equal number of protons in the atoms, which stop the electrons from straying. This is because electrons have a negative charge and protons have a positive charge, and they attract each other. Such materials are called **dielectric**. Other materials, however, have an imbalance of electrons and protons. If they have too few electrons, they have a positive charge. If there are fewer electrons, the material possesses a positive charge. If it has more electrons, the material has a negative charge.

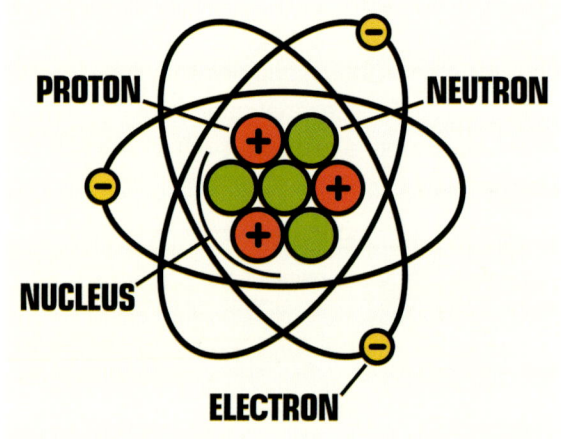

▲ *Materials become charged when they have too many or too few electrons*

Ions

The atoms of some elements can easily lose an electron or two to another atom. Such elements are called metals. When a metal atom loses an electron, it becomes a positively charged ion or cation. Other elements have atoms that are hungry for electrons. When they get an extra electron, they become negatively charged ions or anions. At very high temperatures, cations and anions can form a gas-like material called plasma. All stars are made of this material.

👤 In Real Life

Most clouds are made of plasma, in this case being comprised of charged water ions too, i.e., charged water ions. When these ions come close to the Earth (or to a cloud with ions of opposite charge), they meet an opposite charge and are strongly attracted towards it. The clouds emit a spark, and the excess charge suddenly travels to the Earth, causing lightning.

◀ *Lightning is an example of a static electric discharge*

Electrons

When an electron moves, it produces a tiny **current**. In many metals, electrons can hop between atoms very easily. Some materials are rich in anions, while others are rich in cations. If you bring them together, there will be a chemical reaction. But if you keep them separate and connect them by a wire on one side and an electrode (a metal rod dipped in the substance) on the other side, the current will flow through the wire. This is because electrons will move from the anion-rich side (now called anode) to the cation-rich side (now called cathode). The difference in the charge between the anode and cathode is called the electric potential, which is also often called voltage.

▲ Electric transmission happens when electrons move from an anode (from the power station) to a cathode (back to the power station), through the whole electric grid

Isn't It Amazing!

AC/DC, the name of a famous rock band, does indeed stand for alternating current and direct current. "The band members Malcolm and Angus Young got the idea for the name from their sister, who saw the initials 'AC/DC' on a sewing machine."

Current

Current that flows only in one direction is called direct current or DC. But it can also be made to switch directions, which is called alternating current or AC. The latter happens because of **electromagnetism**. If you rotate a magnet, it creates a tiny electric field. If you put a metal coil around a rotating magnet, the electrons in it will start moving (this is called induction). However, for half a turn, current moves one way, and for the other half it changes direction. The more powerful the magnet, the stronger the current it generates.

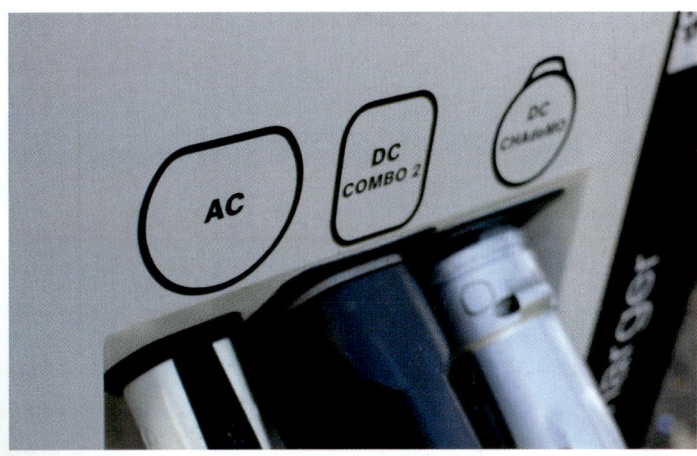

▲ Most devices (such as coffee makers) work either on AC or DC

Current and Resistance

Why does electricity pass through metals, but not other materials? For this, we have to understand the idea of conduction and resistance. **Conduction** happens when there are enough loose electrons that will move when a potential is applied, that is, there is an anode and a cathode between which there is a difference of charge. What if there aren't any electrons to spare, or too many protons hungry for these electrons? Then there will be resistance to the flow of current. These two principles are how most electronic devices work.

▲ Air is a bad conductor, but if two opposite charges enough, it allows a 'spark' to travel between them

Good and Bad Conductors

Most materials will allow some electricity (i.e. some electrons) to pass through them, and resist the rest. A material that lets most of the electrons pass through it is called a good conductor. Most metals are good conductors, and that's why they are used as electric cables. A material that lets all the current pass through it with no resistance at all is called a superconductor. Most good conductors become superconductors only below -253°C, so none of them can be used to make cables that transmit electricity.

On the other hand, bad conductors let little electricity pass through them, which means they resist most electrons. Some materials, like wood and plastics, allow almost no electricity to pass at all. These are called insulators and are used to wrap electric cables so that electricity does not leak out of them.

Yet other materials are neither too bad nor too good and thus they are **semiconductors**. These are important in turning up or turning down the flow of current. Hence, they are the ones that make modern electronics possible.

▲ Insulators protect conductors from leaking electricity and electrocuting people

In Real Life

In theory, your body should be a bad conductor of electricity as 70% of it is made of water (since pure water is a bad conductor of electricity). But it will still let current pass through you, since the body has a lot of salt, which makes it a good conductor. This is why you can get an electric shock. You shouldn't touch an electric device when wet or sweaty as the salt in your skin can conduct electricity.

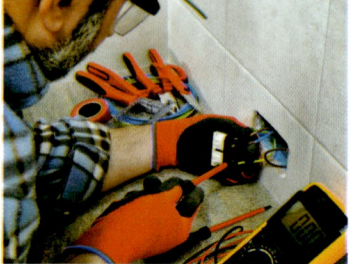

▶ Electricians always work with safety equipment, including insulated gloves, hats, shoes, and glasses

Resistors

So, what happens to electrons as they move along a conductor? Some of them get trapped by positive charges and are lost, reducing the current. This is called resistance (symbol R), and it was worked out by a person called Georg Ohm (1789–1854). The amount of resistance of a conductor can be calculated by measuring the current (symbol I) it lets through and the difference in voltage (symbol V) at either end of the conductor. This is called Ohm's Law, and the unit of resistance is called Ohm (symbol Ω) in his honour.

$$R = V/I$$

Yet other electrons are turned into different forms of electricity. The most common example you see is electric light. Some materials will emit light if current passes through them. This is because as electrons pass through them, they 'excite' the atom and transfer some energy to them. When the electron has passed, the atom becomes 'de-excited' and gives up that energy as a photon, the unit of light. Millions of electrons create millions of photons, and they light up a room. The reverse is also true, and that's how you get solar power. Other resistors turn electricity into heat or sound.

◀ *Electric devices work by converting electrical energy into other forms*

Optic Cables

These cables are used in connecting you to the internet, but they carry light inside them, not electricity. These work on a principle called total internal reflection. They are made of a material (called optical fibre) that reflects photons so that they bounce along the walls all the way from end to end with zero resistance. Hundreds of optical fibres are bundled together to form optical fibre cables (OFCs). These cables are laid all over the world, connecting computers across the globe.

▶ *Optic cables help move millions of bytes of data at the speed of light, all around the world, by turning them into photons*

Making Electricity

We cannot actually make any electricity, because it is a form of energy. As you know, energy can neither be made nor destroyed, but only changed from one form to another. So when we 'generate' electricity, we are only turning some other form of energy into it. In great power plants, this could be thermal, nuclear or mechanical energy; in a battery (cell) or home generator, it is chemical energy which is released by a reaction. Batteries can be rechargeable, such as car batteries; or non-rechargeable, such as in TV remotes, which have to be discarded once exhausted.

▶ Batteries run every portable electronic device, from cars to smart watches

How a Cell Works

Remember that you need an anode and cathode to create an electric potential for electricity to flow. A cell is a device where chemical reactions happen and create the necessary electric potential. Actually, there must be two reactions:

1. The **anode reaction**, which generates electrons that will travel through the electric cables.

2. The **cathode reaction**, which creates a lack of electrons, so that the electric potential is created.

But electricity will not pass unless there is something to connect the anode and cathode internally, so that the cycle is complete. This is called an electrolyte. The electrons come back into the cell, where they meet the cations and neutralise them, i.e. the charge disappears. These electric cycles are called circuits. Many reactions can turn chemical energy into electrical energy this way, but for them to work as a battery, they must be controllable by us.

◀ Batteries come in many sizes and shapes, but all are made of rows of electric cells

In Real Life

A cell is a single unit that produces electricity. However, many cells can be coupled together in rows to increase the total amount of electricity generated. In the 19th century, when inventors worked on these, they were reminded of artillery guns lined up together in a battle. The word for that is 'battery', and that's why a group of cells working together is called a battery.

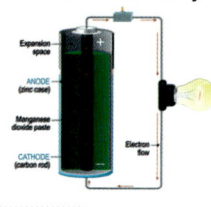

▶ Four lead-acid cells are joined together to make one battery

SCIENCE | ELECTRICITY & ELECTRONICS

Non-Rechargeable Batteries

Most cells cannot be recharged. This is because once the chemical reaction has taken place, it cannot be reversed. Their main advantage is that they are cheap to make and can be made in large numbers, so they are used to power our flashlights, electric toys, music players, and hundreds of other devices. The most common ones use zinc (Zn) as the source of electrons (anode), and manganese dioxide (MnO_2) as the cathode, with a paste of ammonium chloride (NH_4Cl) as the electrolyte. A graphite (carbon) rod is used to take up the electrons, so the cell is also called a zinc-carbon cell.

Dry Cell Battery

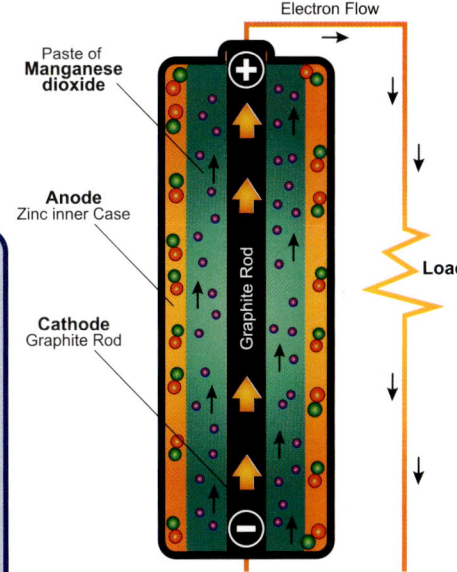

▲ Zinc-carbon cells are among the most commonly used and have a gel-like electrolyte in them

At the anode, zinc releases electrons into the circuit:
$$Zn \rightarrow Zn^{++} + 2e^-$$

At the cathode, the electrons arrive and make manganese dioxide react with ammonium chloride to make manganese trioxide, water and ammonia:
$$2MnO_2 + 2NH_4Cl + 2e^- \rightarrow Mn_2O_3 + 2NH_3 + H_2O + 2Cl^-$$

The chloride ions travel through the electrolyte to react with the zinc ions to make zinc chloride:
$$Zn^{++} + 2Cl^- \rightarrow ZnCl_2$$

Once all the MnO_2 is exhausted, the cell will stop working.

Rechargeable Batteries

Some chemical reactions can be made to run the other way if you apply an electric current to them. This is the principle used in car batteries and other rechargeable ones. The most common is the lead-acid battery, made of alternating plates of lead (symbol Pb) as anode and lead dioxide (symbol PbO_2) as cathode, both dipped in sulphuric acid (symbol H_2SO_4).

▲ Wireless charging of a smartphone battery

Anode reaction: $Pb + H_2SO_4 \rightarrow PbSO_4 + 2H^+ + 2e^-$

The hydrogen ions (H^+) travel to the cathode attracted by the electrons.

Cathode reaction: $PbO_2 + H_2SO_4 + 2H^+ + 2e^- \rightarrow PbSO_4 + 2H_2O$

When the car engine is running, it generates electricity that 'charges' the battery, and the lead and lead dioxide plates regenerate.

Inside a Power Plant

If you thought an electric power plant was just a giant battery, you could be no further from the truth. This is because electric power plants work on induction to generate huge amounts of electricity. But before that, we have to understand the principle of electromagnetism. It is a branch of physics that deals with how electricity and **magnetism** influence each other and is based on the findings of Michael Faraday and James Clerk Maxwell, who discovered that if you move a magnet in an electric field, it will make the electrons in the field move. The reverse is also true. A moving electron creates a tiny magnetic field of its own.

Induction Generator

When a giant magnet is made to rotate inside a metal coil, called an induction coil, it makes an alternating current run through it. This is called an **induction generator**. Lots of these are joined together to make a very large electric current which flows into the **electricity grid** that supplies power to your city. It isn't as simple as we make it out to be, but this is the general principle. Now we come to the question: how do we make the magnet rotate? Engineers attach the blades of a fan to the magnet, which can then be moved by water, wind or steam.

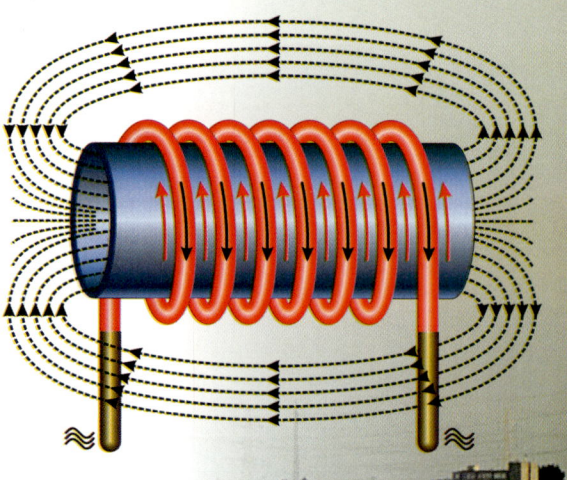

◀ A rotating magnetic field (represented by the dotted arrows) triggers an alternating electric field (represented by the red and black arrows)

▶ Giant power plants are the bedrock of our modern industrial society

Incredible Individuals

Nikola Tesla (1856–1943) made many important inventions that made it possible to produce electricity on a large scale and supply it to homes and factories. His most important invention was the rotating magnet for creating an alternating current. His magnets were installed at the Niagara Falls, where the force of the falling water rotated them.

▶ Serbian-American engineer and physicist Nikola Tesla worked as an employee of Thomas Edison, and later went on to become his rival

Steam Turbines

Wondering why we are talking about steam-driven machines, technology that disappeared nearly a hundred years ago? That's because we still live in the Age of Steam, at least in our power plants. Nuclear and thermal power plants use heat to boil water to make steam, which is then pressurised and passed into a chamber. The steam turns the wings of giant turbines that, in turn, rotate a magnet inside an induction coil, thereby generating electricity.

The heat for making steam comes in two ways: thermal power plants burn fuel such as coal or gas to generate heat, while nuclear power plants use a **nuclear reaction** to generate heat. A nuclear reaction is one in which a radioactive material, like uranium, breaks up to release energy (as heat), while turning into a new element.

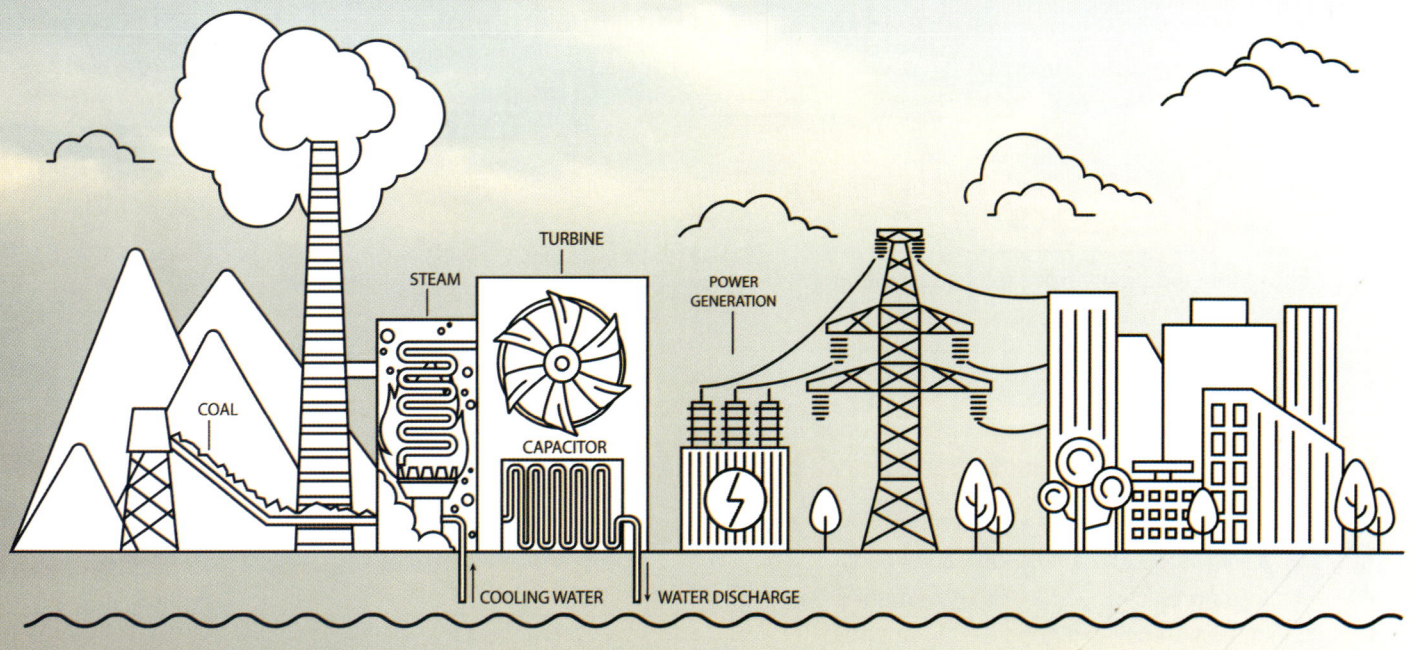

▲ *The parts of a thermal power plant: Coal is burned to turn water into steam, which then flows through turbines to make electricity*

Isn't It Amazing!

Dams use the power of falling water to turn the turbines which turn the rotor. China's Three Gorges Dam, with 34 generators, is the world's largest dam.

Capacitors

You know how a cell works. Now take the electrolyte of a cell, and replace it with a dielectric medium, one that conducts no current (see page 6). Run electricity into the cell. The anode and cathode will simply build up a charge, looking for somewhere to discharge it. Instead of a cell, you now have a capacitor. Capacitors are a big part of grids as they store the electricity generated in power plants. The amount of electricity a capacitor can store is called capacitance (symbol C, unit Farad [F]). When there is 'demand', that is when millions of people switch on a device at home, the capacitors are plugged into the network. Now that the circuit is complete, the electrons rush out of the anode to the cathode of the capacitor.

▲ *Banks of capacitors are called electric substations*

Electric Circuits

We've learned how power is generated from other sources of energy. But electricity only moves as a current if it can complete a circuit from the power source and back to it. On the way it will meet various kinds of resistors and other devices that will convert electrical energy to other forms of energy, which we use for our purposes—such as lighting and cooling a room, or powering TVs and computers. Some of the electricity will be used to power a motor (see pages 16–17). But not all devices use the same amount of electricity, nor do they need to be switched on all the time.

▼ Transformers at a power station

Transformers

In most countries, electricity travels through metal cables high in the air or underground at electric potentials of up to 765,000 volts, or 765 kilovolts (V and kV respectively). However, when it has to be connected to your home, it needs to be reduced to as little as 440V. For that, it needs a transformer.

▲ The magnetic field generated by one coil affects the other, triggering a current in it

Transformers act on electricity like the volume controls on a TV remote, by a method you already know—electromagnetic induction. But now there's a twist. If an induction coil is placed next to another (without touching) and alternating current is passed through it, there will be a new current in the other coil! The current in that coil depends on the number of turns there are in that coil. So, if you have a coil with more turns than the first one, it will have more current. In this manner, you will have made a step-up transformer. If there are fewer turns in the coil than the first one, then you have a step-down transformer. Power companies pass the electricity they generate through several step-up transformers before it is loaded onto the electricity grid. The power from the grid passes through many of these before reaching your home.

Switches

A switch works in the simplest way—by breaking the circuit mechanically. Each light in your house is connected to the power grid by its own circuit. When you turn it off, the switch moves the cables away, and the device goes off. When you turn it on, the switch reconnects the circuit, and your device comes on. For gadgets like blenders or televisions, the switch is made by a power socket, into which you must plug in your device and then turn on the switch. The device's cable acts as a second switch.

▼ This is how electric switches work

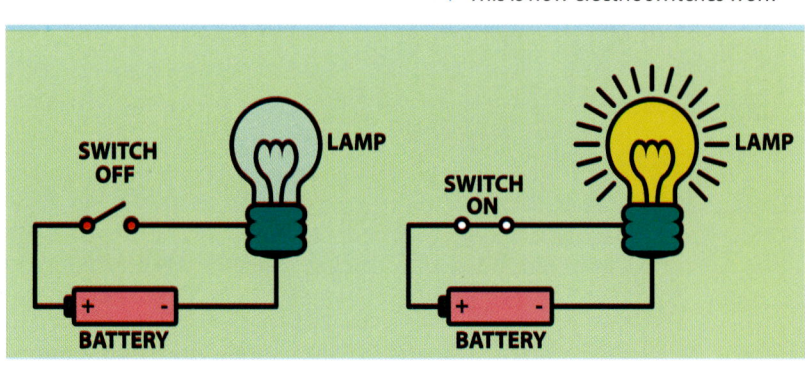

Series and Parallel

If you split a power cable, connect it to two electric devices, and then link up their cables back again, you create a **parallel circuit**. If you connect both electric devices to the same circuit, one after the other, you have made a **series circuit**. However, in a series circuit, if one device fails, it will turn the other one off too.

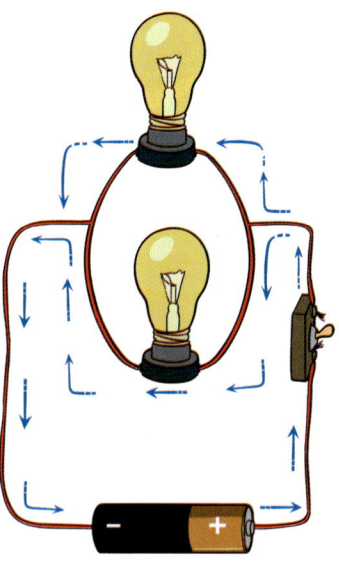

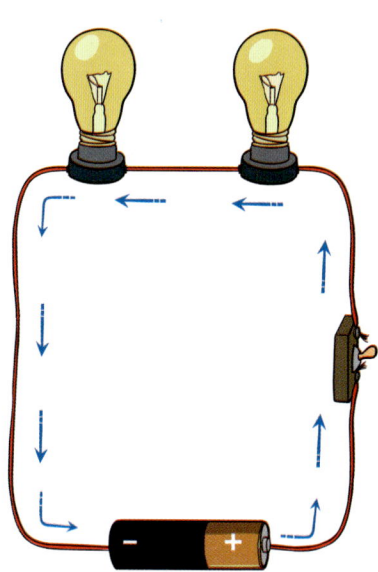

▲ *Parallel connections make sure that one device can keep running even if the other fails, as it doesn't break the circuit*

Isn't It Amazing!

String lights, which have dozens of little lights in series, actually work in parallel circuits. That's why even if one light goes bad, the whole string does not go dark.

▶ *Hanging string lights used for various occasions*

In Real Life

Your home's bell is one of the simplest applications of electromagnetism. When you press the bell, electricity runs through a coil wrapped around a metal bar or horseshoe, magnetising it. It attracts another metal rod, which hits a gong. In doing so, it breaks the circuit, the magnetism stops and the rod goes back to its place.

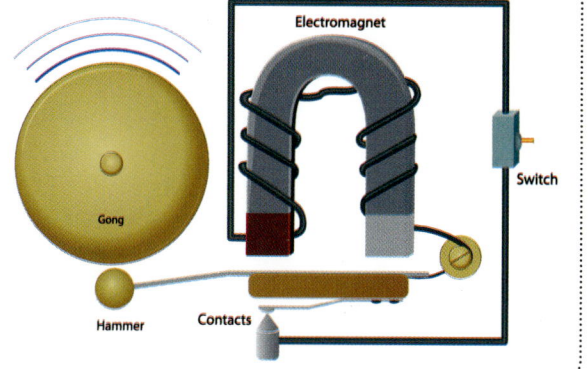

▶ *The magnetic field generated by one coil affects the other, triggering a current in it*

Motors and Magnetism

There are two ways by which electricity is put to work. One you know already—using resistors to turn electricity into heat, light or sound. Another way is by induction, but this time the other way around. Passing electricity through a coil makes a magnet rotate. The rotating magnet can be fixed to other things to make them rotate too. This is the principle of the **electric motor**. You see them in familiar devices and day-to-day life, such as blenders, fans, and lawnmowers; but they also work in not-so-familiar devices such as mechanical toys, chainsaws, water pumps, electric trains, and cars, and a whole lot of industrial machinery.

▲ An electric motor with its various parts

▼ An electric motor winding

⭐ Incredible Individuals

The Hungarian monk and school teacher Anyos Jedlik invented one of the world's earliest working motors back in 1827.

🔍 Parts of a Motor

Every electric motor has two essential parts: one stationary and one that rotates. The stationary part of an electric motor, called the stator, has the electric coils. When electricity is run through it, it creates a magnetic field. The rotor is the metallic rod or shaft that rotates in response to the magnetic field created by the live stator. Ball bearings usually anchor the rotor to the motor's casing and help it rotate. A tiny device called commutator is present between the rotor and the stator, and is responsible for the conversion of direct current into alternating current.

👤 In Real Life

An electrical device, cable, or coil is said to be "live" when electricity is passing through it, and dormant otherwise. Electric transmission lines are live all the time, as are the electric boxes you see in substations and in your house's fuse box. This is why you should never touch them.

▲ Live power lines are usually kept away from populated areas

SCIENCE — ELECTRICITY & ELECTRONICS

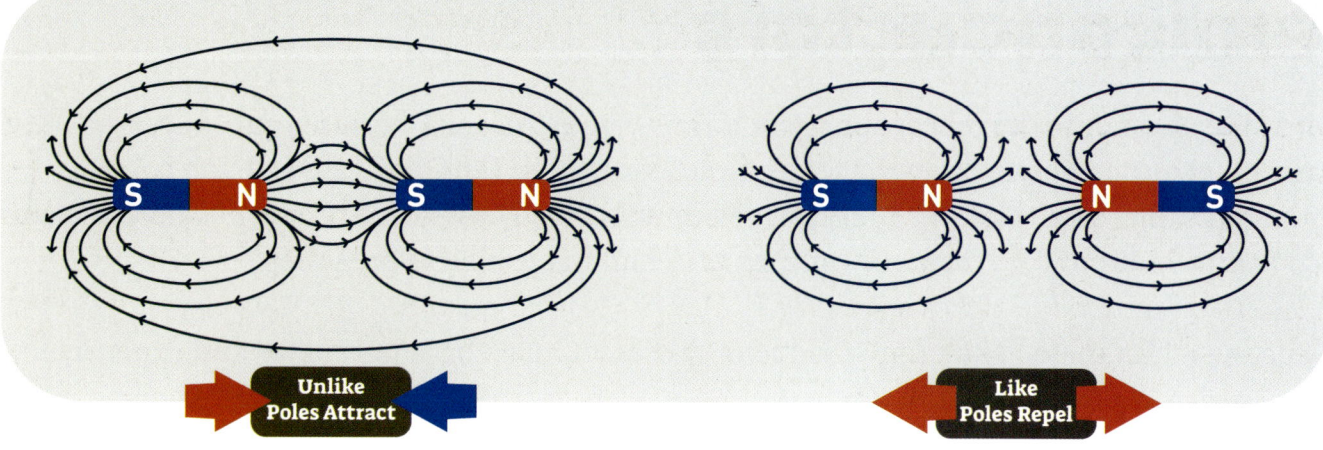

Unlike Poles Attract

Like Poles Repel

⚡ ELECTROMAGNETISM ⚡

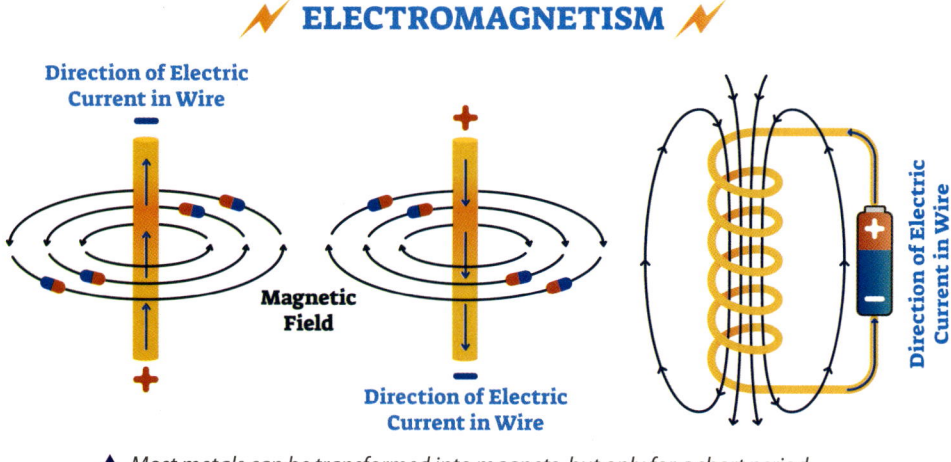

The Earth's Magnetic Field

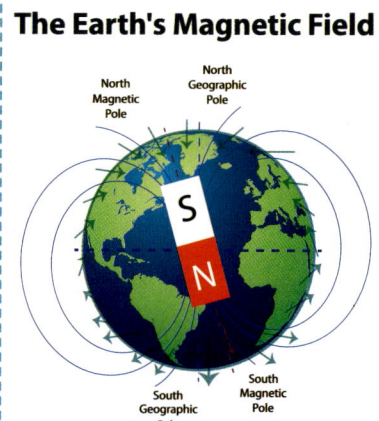

▲ Most metals can be transformed into magnets, but only for a short period

Magnetism

We've talked much about electricity causing a magnetic field, and the reverse. But what exactly is magnetism? Why do some materials, like iron, show it, and others, like copper, do not?

A magnetic field is a force produced at a right angle to the movement of a charge. Magnetic forces move within that field between its north and south poles (this field is called a dipole). The way opposite electric charges attract, opposite magnetic poles attract. And just as 'like' electric charges repel each other, like magnetic poles repel.

In most materials, electrons move in all directions, so their magnetic fields cancel each other out. These materials are called **diamagnetic**. However, in other materials such as good conductors, applying an electric charge can make all the electrons move in one direction, and so they get a magnetic field, though it does not last for long—These are **paramagnetic**. Lastly, in materials such as iron, the magnetic fields can be permanent if the current is run for a long time—These are **ferromagnetic**. Permanent magnets, like the ones seafarers use in a magnetic compass, are made of these.

💡 Isn't It Amazing!

Our planet's core is made of a solid iron ball surrounded by molten iron. As the Earth rotates, this molten iron (which is charged) also moves, creating a gigantic magnetic field that covers the whole planet. It is roughly the same as the Earth's axis of rotation but is off by a few hundred miles. The North Magnetic Pole is is in the Canadian Arctic moving towards Russia, while the South Magnetic Pole is located off the coast of Antarctica.

▲ Powerful horseshoe magnets are used in recycling yards to separate metals from non-metals

Semiconductors

Look at the electronic devices around you today—smartphones, laptops, automatic washing machines, programmable microwaves, remote-controlled fans and LEDs. If you ask your grandparents, fifty years ago the 'smartest' device out there would have been a pocket calculator, which is now reduced to an app on your phone. What made all this possible?

The answer is that these are all semiconductor devices. Once, these were large and expensive devices, which could do only the simplest of programming tasks. But as we learned more about them, we learned to fit more and more electronic circuits into a smaller space on a semiconductor **chip**. These devices became smaller and cheaper, and several of us own devices with semiconductors today.

What are semiconductors?

Silicon, selenium, and germanium are all examples of semiconductor materials. They have too few 'loose' electrons to be good conductors, but enough of them to not be insulators. In the last two centuries, physicists discovered that their partial conduction of electricity could be useful to regulate how it flowed, and to use them as 'gates' in a circuit. This means they can make electrons flow in one direction and stop them from another. Further, they can combine two streams of electrons into one; they can 'decide' to let one current pass instead of another, and so on. Using this, they can be programmed to do tasks like doing sums or control other electronic devices.

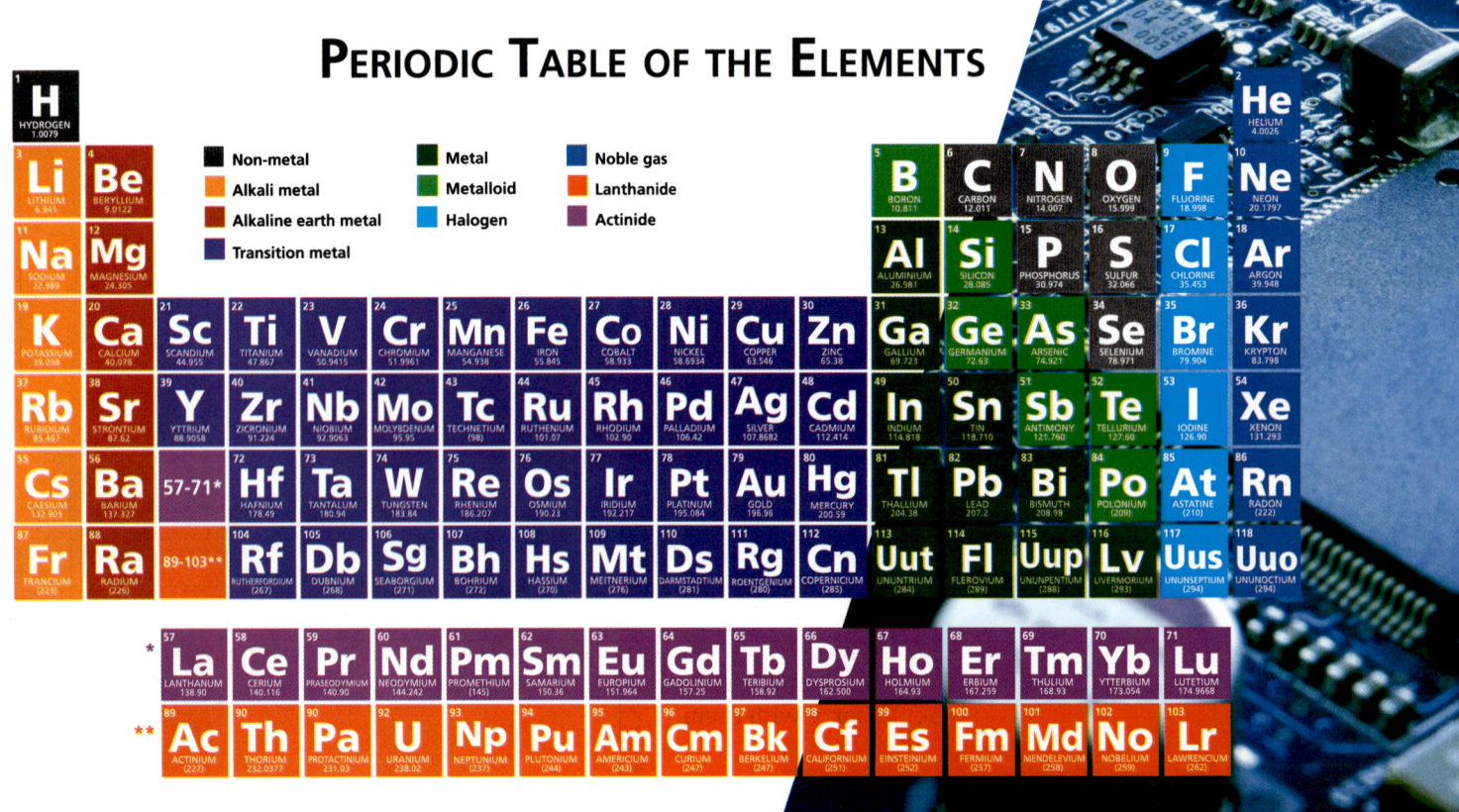

▲ *Elements marked in light green make good semiconductors. Those in dark green and grey are used for doping*

Doping

In the 20th century, many scientists who worked together discovered that semiconductors can be 'doped'. By doping, they mean that a pure semiconductor crystal could be deliberately adulterated with another material that increases or decreases the amount of electricity that it can conduct. If you add small amounts of phosphorus (5 electrons to spare) to silicon (4 electrons to spare), you get an **n-doped** semiconductor, which has a slight negative charge. Similarly, by adding boron (3 electrons to spare) to silicon, you get a **p-doped** semiconductor with a slight positive charge. Now, by putting the two together, you get a **p-n junction**. If you run a small current with n first and p later, the current will flow easily, but if you reverse the current, it does not go past p, as it takes up the electrons to make up for the ones it is missing. Thus, a p-n junction acts like a one-way gate.

P–N JUNCTION

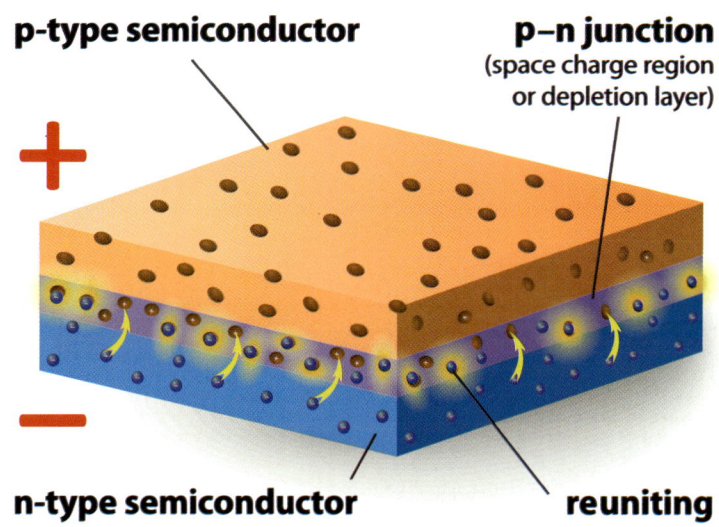

▲ p–n junctions are used as gates in electronic circuits

Transistors

What if we make complicated junctions such as n-p-n or p-n-p? We can make another device called a transistor. This device controls how much electricity can flow through it, by using a second current to modify the conductivity of one of the semiconductors. The incoming power is called the source, and the outgoing power is called the drain. The part of the transmitter that receives the source is called the collector, while the part from which the drain leaves is called the emitter. Between them is a third connection, called the base (which receives the 'gate' current) that adjusts the conductivity. You can thus use transistors as tiny transformers to increase or decrease signal.

▲ A transistor with the source, gate and drain

Isn't It Amazing!

John Bardeen, Walter H. Brattain, and William B. Shockley invented semiconductor transistors. Their first use was in making 'pocket' radios, which people could carry with them.

▶ To most people in the 1960s and 1970s, a transistor meant a pocket radio

Diodes and Displays

In electronics, a diode is a device which offers high resistance when current is passed one way, and low resistance the other way. You've already seen how p-n junctions work; they make the best diodes. Before that, diodes were made of a glass tube, in which a rod-shaped cathode and a plate-shaped anode were fitted with a vacuum in between. Electricity can only pass from cathode to anode; if you plug in the diode the other way, it will stop the circuit.

These big diodes (and related devices called triodes, which acted as transistors) were used in building the first electronic circuits in which electricity could be put to use in making calculations, keeping track of time and other things. Diodes can deduct electrons or add them. Multiple diodes can conduct more complex jobs. In the 1950s, the vacuum tubes (which would break down easily) were replaced by semiconductor diodes. Over time, these diodes were reduced in size, becoming smaller and smaller to such an extent that today thousands of diodes (and transistors) can be fitted onto a silicon chip smaller than a fingernail! This is called a microprocessor.

▲ *The first diodes were vacuum tubes, which would easily go bust. Today's diodes are tiny and much more reliable*

LED Lighting

White light is made by mixing several colours. Another method of making white light is by using phosphor, a substance that absorbs light of one colour and emits another. Tube lights and compact fluorescent lamps work on the same principle. In an LED lamp, a blue LED emits light, which falls on the phosphor that has been coated inside the light. It absorbs some of the light and emits yellow light. The yellow light mixes with the remaining blue light to make white light.

▼ *Streets lit with LED lights save your municipality a lot of money*

Light-emitting Diode

Some p-n semiconductor junction diodes emit light when electricity passes through them. This is the principle used in LED lamps, that are fast replacing the earlier incandescent and fluorescent lamps. They are brighter and need a lot less electric power, although they may also be more expensive. The LED technology is also used in making screens of TVs, computers, touch phones and other devices.

Different combinations (dopes) of semiconductors emit lights of different colours (see the table below). A multicolour LED display is made of several such tiny diodes.

Light Colour	Combination
Red	Aluminium gallium arsenide (AlGaAs)
Orange	Gallium arsenide phosphide (GaAsP)
Yellow	Aluminium gallium indium phosphide (AlGaInP)
Green	Gallium (III) nitride (GaN)
Blue	Zinc selenide (ZnSe)

Other colours can be obtained by placing different colour LEDs in the same diode, as per the colour chart.

▲ LED lights in many colours at an airport

Isn't It Amazing!

The world's largest LED 3D screen was installed in Gothenburg in 2011 to show fans the Union of European Football Associations (UEFA) Cup final (which happened in London), where Barcelona beat Manchester United 3–1. The screen measured 6,192 mm by 3,483 mm.

 LED Display

Most screens, whether in TVs, phones, or computers, are switching to LED displays. This works by putting three microscopic LEDs into a **pixel**, which is the unit of space in all digital screens. These LEDs give off red, blue, and green light when live. When a digital signal comes into the screen, it has information for each pixel—which LEDs need to be switched on and with how much intensity. This leads to the various colours and pictures that we see on the screen.

▶ The more pixels on an LED screen, the sharper the image displayed

Interesting Electrical Phenomena

Alongside magnetism, there are other phenomena which can generate electric currents. Some are useful to us and can power gadgets, while others can create problems that we have to be careful about.

Piezoelectricity is a phenomenon when electricity is generated in some types of crystals when they are pressed.

Triboelectricity occurs when two materials are rubbed together, causing charged particles to appear on their surface.

Pyroelectricity is the property of some materials to generate a voltage difference when heated or cooled.

Thermoelectricity is a phenomenon that happens when two different materials, with different electric and thermal conductivity, are joined together. A difference in temperature between them also leads to a difference in voltage.

Let's look at some of these in detail, and how scientists and engineers use them to generate electricity and make many kinds of devices work.

▼ As electricity is a form of energy, any other kind of energy can be converted into it, using the right materials

Piezoelectricity

Piezoelectricity (*piezo* is 'to press' in Greek) was discovered by the brothers Jacques Curie and Pierre Curie (husband of Marie Curie) in 1880. They demonstrated that if you put pressure on crystals of tourmaline, quartz, and even sugar, they will generate a tiny electric current. It also works the other way round—a current passed through these crystals can cause them to deform. The piezoelectric effect is used in many devices, such as electric balances for weighing diamonds, guitar pick-ups, electronic drums, and kitchen lighters. Scientists are trying to figure out a way to use the piezoelectric effect to make electricity from car tyres.

▶ When you push the lighter button, it strikes a piezoelectric crystal which generates a tiny current, which in turn creates a spark that ignites the gas

Triboelectricity

Triboelectricity (*tribo* is 'to rub' in Greek) happens when two charged surfaces rub against each other, such as running a comb through hair or rubbing a glass with fur. Triboelectricity is the main source of static electricity. The rubbing causes electrons to come loose on the surface of the material. When an electrically conductive surface (like your skin) comes in touch with the charged material, the electrons travel onto it. This causes a mild electric shock.

Triboelectricity is the reason rockets are not launched during storms. In a storm, the air is full of charged particles, and if the rocket rubbed past them, the static electricity generated would interfere with the radio signals between the rocket and the control centre.

▲ *The triboelectric effect can also affect electronic chips as the static voltage caused by accidental rubbing of the chip can overwhelm the tiny currents of the chips*

Pyroelectricity

Pyroelectricity (*pyro* is 'fire' in Greek) is a phenomenon seen in certain kinds of crystals, like gallium nitride. When the crystal is heated even by a tiny amount, it generates an electric current, because the increased vibration caused by heating the molecules causes them to shed electrons. The pyroelectric effect is used in infrared sensors, in which the heat given off in the form of infrared electromagnetic waves can be captured by the sensor. These are used in automatic switches, which can turn the lights on or off in a room by sensing your presence through your body heat. They are also used in camera traps for photographing wild animals.

▶ *An infrared camera trap can sense the heat of an animal when it comes close to it and trigger the camera to take a photograph*

Thermoelectric Effect

The thermoelectric effect (*thermo* is 'heat' in Greek) was discovered by Thomas Seebeck in 1821. He noticed that two metals that are joined at the ends will have different electric conductivity because of the difference in their heat conductivity. This is also known as the Seebeck effect.

Scientists use this principle to build electronic thermometers using a device called a thermocouple made of wires of different metals or alloys. Thermocouples are very sensitive to even slight differences in temperature, and can also be used for measuring very high temperatures, such as in gas stoves or in the furnaces of factories where metals are refined from their ores.

▶ *The long wire you see is the thermocouple which senses the temperature, which the device then converts into a digital display*

Analogue and Digital

Engineers divide measurements into two kinds—analogue and digital. Analogue things are those that come in continuous measures, such as time, space, temperature, or speed. When you measure them, you can express the measurements in decimals. For instance, your body's normal temperature is 37.5°C, acceleration due to the Earth's gravity is 9.80665 m/s^2 and so on. Analogue devices, such as the mercury thermometer or a clock with gears, measure these things on a continuous basis.

On the other hand, digital things are those that come in whole numbers. The most common digital things are light waves and sound waves, because there cannot be such a thing as half a wave. After the introduction of **quantum theory**, we know that many natural forces are actually discrete, that is, they come in quanta, because they are made up of particles. Electricity is made of moving electrons; light (including X-rays and Gamma rays) is made of photons; and nuclear radiation is made of alpha or beta particles.

Electronic engineers therefore face a puzzle. Most of their measurements are in analogue, but the tools they make to measure them are digital. Converting analogue signals to digital ones that can be displayed takes up much of their time.

In Real Life

We often use analogue as a shorthand for things that are not electronic, and digital for those that are. But many non-electronic things, such as cameras that use film, are also digital. The camera film is made of molecules, and each molecule carries colour information, which makes it digital at a fundamental level.

▲ *An analogue watch shows time as it passes, whereas a digital watch can show you the time only once every second*

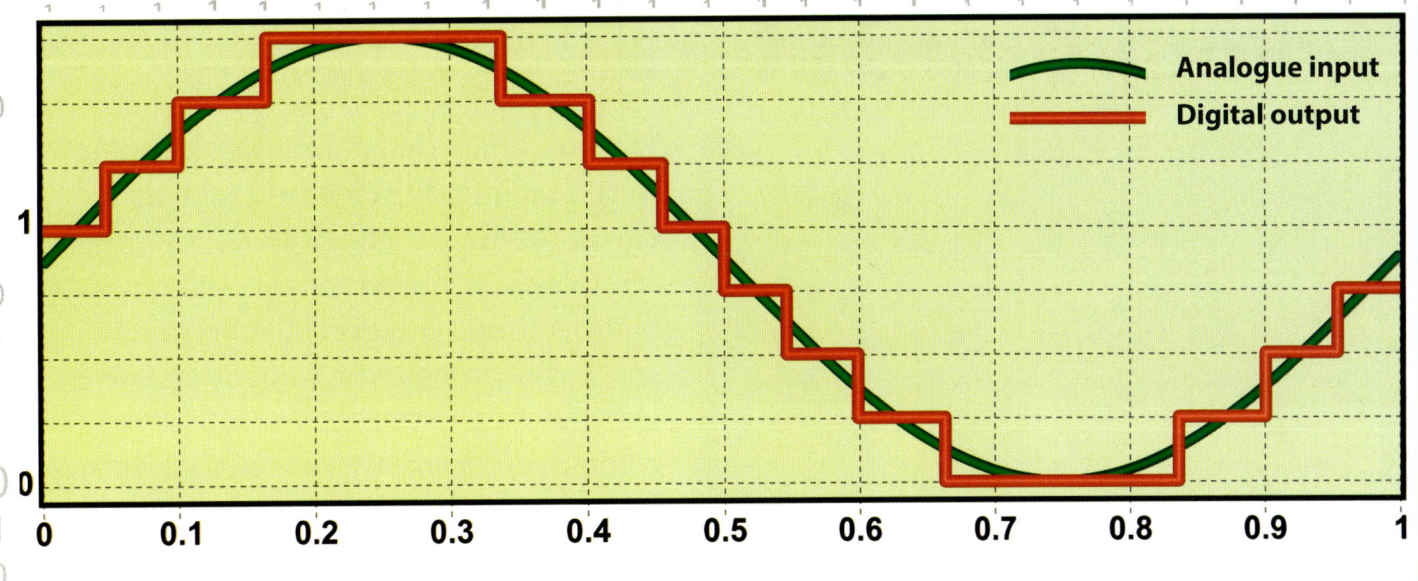

▲ Analogue-to-digital conversion turns a continuous measure into a discrete one

🔍 Analogue to Digital Conversion

Digital (derived from the Latin word 'digit', which means 'finger', that we all use to count) means that any measure, that engineers call a signal, has to be represented as an integer (i.e. a number that can be counted on the fingers). Therefore, a digital device can only 'sample' a continuous signal and produce snippets of that signal (see above image). This is called analogue-to-digital conversion. For electronic engineers, this means that to get a digital signal which represents the original as accurately as possible, they need to become more and more precise, so that the smallest changes in the analogue signal can be picked up. This is important where many decisions have to be made at very high speeds, such as in a radar detecting a flying plane.

They do this by trying to build sensors that are extremely small through a process called **miniaturisation**. With our improved understanding of semiconductors, we have been able to build devices on very small scales. Today, with nanotechnology, we can go down to the molecular level and get as accurate a signal as is physically possible.

🔍 Digital to Analogue Conversion

Digital displays face a different problem—turning a digital signal into an analogue one, so that we can make sense of them. Otherwise we wouldn't be able to hear our friends on the phone or see an image on the TV. Engineers solve this, again, through miniaturisation, and that's why you see TVs and cameras sold based on megapixels. A pixel is a unit of space which counts as one digital unit; a megapixel is one million pixels. The smaller the pixel, the better the resolution of a digital image.

▼ The more pixels (digital units of space) an image packs, the sharper it is

Making Computers

Did you know that computers in the 1950s were so big that they would take up an entire room? It is only with the invention of semiconductor-based diodes and transistors that electronic circuits could become smaller, allowing more computing power to be built up in the same space. Over time, computers became as small as a cupboard (mainframe), to a device that could sit on your table (desktop), and then on your lap (laptop). Now the device fits in your palm and is called a smartphone. But there's more to them getting smaller than just the microprocessor.

▲ *Early computers took up entire rooms and had lesser computing power than your mobile phone*

Integrated Circuit

An integrated circuit (IC) puts transistors, resistors, diodes, and capacitors—all microscopic in size—onto a semiconductor chip. After an engineer designs the circuit, it is printed onto a chip by a method called photolithography. Conducting metal strips are laid onto the chip, while other areas are modified chemically to make n-p junctions.

Data Storage

For a computer to work, it must be able to store data in a device called a **memory chip**. All data is stored as bits—a simple binary signal in a computer circuit that is either on (1) or off (0). Eight bits make a byte. Read Only Memory (ROM) stores data permanently, while Random Access Memory (RAM) stores the data temporarily while doing calculations. This is the same as how you hold 1,245 in your head while you try to mentally add 6,567 to it: you need to remember the places (tens, hundreds, thousands) of the digits. The processing power of a computer is usually expressed in terms of the total number of bytes its RAM has.

▲ *An electronic circuit board has dozens of IC-chips pasted onto it along with other microelectronics*

◄ *Data storage devices have evolved over time, from paper tapes, cellulose film, magnetic (floppy) discs, and compact discs to modern micro SD cards*

In Real Life

In 1965, Gordon Moore, a computer scientist, predicted that the number of transistors on a microprocessor would double each year. He turned out to be nearly right, since they do double roughly once every 18 months. This is now called Moore's Law. Today, over 23 billion transistors can fit onto one chip!

SCIENCE | ELECTRICITY & ELECTRONICS

Programming

An algorithm or programme is a set of steps that the computer follows to know what it has to do. Thousands of algorithms are needed to run your computer smoothly (the **operating system**), while others come bundled in packages that help you do calculations, process natural languages (word processors), connect to the internet, listen to music or watch movies—these are called **applications**. Together, they are called **software**, while the physical parts of the computer (or smartphone) are known as **hardware**. The science of creating algorithms is called programming. In most modern computers, programming is done through various codes called **computer languages**. They come in two main categories: Low Level Languages and High Level Languages. The first type mainly interact with the hardware of computers, helping in operations and handling instructions by converting input into machine language—1 and 0. The second comprise of programming languages for different utilities and purposes such as Java, C++, FORTRAN, PASCAL, and Python.

Incredible Individuals

Ada Lovelace (1815–1852) left behind a step-by-step manual of how to calculate a complex kind of number called a 'Bernoulli number' for which a new kind of device—the Analytical Engine—was to be built by her friend, Charles Babbage, in 1843. For this, she is celebrated as the first programmer ever. The second Tuesday of every October is celebrated as Ada Lovelace Day.

▲ Ada Lovelace

▼ The world's first-ever computer programme, created by Ada Lovelace in 1843

Mobile Phones

When we say 'phone' today, a little rectangular object that can connect to the internet and search for information, and contains messaging apps and social networks, comes to mind. But if you ever saw a telephone from the 1970s or '80s, you would wonder how it should be used.

▶ The telephones of older times, invented by Alexander Graham Bell and patented in 1876, look nothing like the modern telephones we use today

🔍 Speaking and Listening

So how does a smartphone work? Inside most mobile phones, you'll find the following six things: a central processing unit, an LED display, a microphone, a speaker, a camera, and a battery to power them all. The microphone is made of a tiny magnetic membrane called a **diaphragm**. When you speak, sound waves from your mouth reach the diaphragm and make it vibrate. As it vibrates, it triggers electric current in an **electrode** just next to it, which passes through an analogue-to-digital convertor and becomes a digital signal. This signal is then sent to the mobile network, which sends it to your friend's phone.

In your friend's phone, the digital signal passes through a digital-to-analogue convertor and then a tiny electromagnet. The magnet attracts or repels another diaphragm. The movement of this diaphragm makes sound waves in the air, which reach your friend's ear as an analogue signal. Most telephones are quite precise, but not perfect, so sometimes people sound different in real life and over the phone.

▲ A modern mobile phone network

SCIENCE | ELECTRICITY & ELECTRONICS

◀ A modern mobile phone with multitasking applications

▶ A modern mobile phone tower

🔍 Sending and Receiving

Your phone has an in-built antenna, which converts the digital signal into a radio wave. Before that, the **Subscriber Identity Module (SIM)** card in your phone tacks on a code that helps the network identify you and where you are. The signal reaches the telephone tower or base station nearest to you, where it is again converted into an electric signal that can travel by cable, or into a more powerful radio signal that is transmitted to a communication satellite. It then passes through many telephone exchanges, which identify the receiver's number and switch them onto the right path (which is why telephone numbers have a country and an area code before your actual number). Finally, the signal reaches the cell your friend is in, and a radio signal passes to their phone, which rings. The geographic area served by each base station is called a cell, and that's why the whole process is referred to as cellular telephony.

⭐ Incredible Individuals

Before the telephone, there was the telegraph, a device that sent signals over long cables. Your message (in writing) had to be encoded into a series of short and long beeps called Morse code, and the code then had to be decoded at the other end. People who did this were called telegraph operators. In 1866, Mathilde Fibiger became one of the first women to be hired for the job, which was earlier thought to be suitable only for men.

▶ Mathilde Fibiger (bottom) and the telegraph equipment she would have used (top).

Renewable Energy

In the last few decades, people around the world have become concerned with what is happening to the wonderful nature and environment around us. Human activities are stuffing the air with millions of tonnes of carbon dioxide and causing climate change, plastics are polluting the ocean, and pesticides and other chemicals are killing insects and other wildlife. The generation of electricity is one of the biggest causes of climate change—from thermal power plants that emit CO_2, to the big dams that cause a lot of harm to the ecology around them. On the other hand, nuclear power is not leading to pollution, but it poses a threat if there is a leakage of radioactive material. Another problem is the fuel used for nuclear and thermal plants, which is expected to exhaust one day. That is why scientists and engineers across the world have been trying to find ways to generate electricity from a fuel source that will not run out or pollute the Earth.

★ Incredible Individuals

In 1962, the marine biologist Rachel Carson published the book *Silent Spring*, which warned of the dangers caused to the environment by modern industry. The book inspired many people to think of ways to reduce our impact on Earth, and was a great inspiration for people researching renewable energy.

▲ *Rachel Carson's book inspired many people to work on renewable energy*

🔍 Solar Power

This power depends on a source of energy that will eventually run out, but only after a few billion years. Light from the Sun is renewed every day and we can easily turn it into electricity. The device that does this is called a photovoltaic cell. It is made of silicon crystals. When photons from sunlight fall on the silicon crystals, the electrons in them become 'excited'. If these crystals are connected to an electrical circuit, these excited electrons start moving, forming an electric current. Solar is increasingly becoming popular as an alternative to conventional energy production.

▲ *Solar panels, made of solar cells, make the wings of satellites and give them the electricity they need*

Wind Power

People, in order to create energy, especially for running flourmills, have long been using windmills. In the 20th century, as turbine technology improved, windmills were used for generating electricity. In a place that's extremely windy, the blades of the fan would automatically move, and a turbine would then convert this motion into electricity.

Geothermal Power

▲ Traditional windmills

The earth releases heat from its interiors to its surface through **volcanism**. In many places (such as Iceland) this heat makes ground water escape as steam (making a geyser) or turns it **super hot** if trapped inside. A geothermal power plant captures the released steam and makes it run through a turbine to produce electricity. In other places where steam does not escape naturally, a pipe is drilled to reach the water. As the water rises, it turns into steam because the pressure falls, and is directed to turn a turbine. The steam is condensed and pumped back into the earth, where it can be heated again.

▲ A geyser in Strokkur, Iceland

Tidal Power

Tidal power uses the energy stored in tides as they rise and fall. Tidal power engineers build a dam that captures water when the tide rises. When the tide recedes, the gates of the dam open and the water flows out into the sea. As it flows, it turns a turbine. In other places, the natural ocean current is directly used to move a turbine.

▶ Modern windmills

▶ A tidal barrage with turbines

Word Check

Anode: The part of a cell that generates anions (gives off electrons)

Anode reaction: The chemical reaction in a cell that gives off electrons

Application: A set of programmes that helps a computer to do a certain task

Cathode: The part of a cell that generates cations (needs electrons)

Cathode reaction: The chemical reaction in a cell that takes up electrons

Chip: A tiny plate of semiconducting material onto which an integrated circuit is printed

Computer language: A set of codes in which computer algorithms can be written

Conduction: The passage of electricity through a material

Current: The movement of electrons across an electric potential.

Current electricity: Electricity that moves across an electric potential

Diamagnetic: Materials that cannot be magnetised at all

Diaphragm: A thin membrane that vibrates when sound waves fall on it

Dielectric: A substance that does not allow current to pass

Diode: An electronic device that allows current to pass in one direction only

Electric charge: An excess or lack of electrons in a material. It is measured in Coulombs

Electric motor: A device that converts electrical energy into mechanical energy through induction

Electricity grid: A network of electric cables and power plants that supplies power to a city or country

Electrode: A device that conducts electricity into a circuit (anode), or away from it (cathode)

Electromagnetism: An electric field created by a moving magnet, or a magnetic field created by a moving electron

Ferromagnetic: Materials that can be magnetised permanently

Gate current : An additional current in a transistor that increases or decreases its conductivity

Hardware: The physical parts that make up a computer or other smart devices

Induction generator: A device that produces electricity by magnetic induction

Magnetism: A condition in some metals in which the electrons move in the same direction

Memory chip: A semiconductor chip used for saving data in magnetic form

Miniaturisation: The process by which digital sensors and displays are made smaller to reflect the analogue world

N-dope: A non-metallic dope added to a semiconductor to make it relatively negatively charged.

Nuclear reaction: A reaction by which the nuclei of atoms give out energy by splitting apart

Operating system: The set of programmes that are needed to run a computer smoothly

P-dope: A metallic dope added to a semiconductor to make it relatively positively charged.

P-n junction: A diode made by putting together small crystals of p-doped and n-doped semiconductors together.

Parallel circuit: A circuit in which various devices are connected parallel to each other

Paramagnetic: Materials that can be magnetised for a short while

Pixel: The digital unit of space used to convert analogue images into digital ones

Quantum Theory: The fundamental theory of physics that electromagnetic forces are made of discrete particles that may be charged (e.g. electrons) or not (e.g. photons)

Semiconductor: A material that allows only some electricity to pass through it

Series circuit: A circuit in which various devices are connected one after another

Software: The operating system and applications used in a computer or smartphone

Static electricity: Electricity that is created by a build-up of charge

Subscriber Identity Module (SIM): A silicon chip that carries a code identifying a user, which is added to the mobile signal during each call

Super hot water: Water that has been heated above 100°C, but has not turned to steam because of extreme pressure

Turbine: A device rotated by flowing liquid or gas

Volcanism: Release of energy, mostly as heat, from within the earth